PANINI COOKBOOK

Step-by-step recipes for making delicious panini at home

TABLE OF CONTENTS

utter responsibility of the recipient reader. Under no circumstances will any legal responsibility or blame be held against the publisher for any reparation, damages, or monetary loss due to the information herein, either directly or indirectly.

Respective authors own all copyrights not held by the publisher.

The information herein is offered for informational purposes solely, and is universal as so. The presentation of the information is without contract or any type of guarantee assurance.

The trademarks that are used are without any consent, and the publication of the trademark is without permission or backing by the trademark owner. All trademarks and brands within this book are for clarifying purposes only and are the owned by the owners themselves, not affiliated with this document.

Introduction

Panini recipes for personal enjoyment but also for family enjoyment. You will love them for sure for how easy it is to prepare them.

BREAKFAST PANINI

Serves: 2
Prep Time: 5   Minutes
Cook Time: 5   Minutes
Total Time: *10* Minutes

INGREDIENTS

- ¼ tsp salt
- 1 cup cheese
- 1 package bacon
- 4 slices bread
- 1 fried egg

DIRECTIONS

1. Prepare bread for the panini
2. Place all the ingredients on a bread slice
3. Top with the other bread slice
4. Toast panini until golden brown

5. Serve when ready

BISTRO BREAKFAST PANINI

Serves: **2**
Prep Time: **5**   Minutes
Cook Time: **5**   Minutes
Total Time: **10** Minutes

INGREDIENTS

- 4 bacon strips
- 1 tsp butter
- 2 eggs
- 4 slices bread
- ¼ tsp salt
- 2 oz. cheese
- ¼ cup baby spinach

DIRECTIONS

1. Prepare bread for the panini
2. Place all the ingredients on a bread slice

3. Top with the other bread slice
4. Toast panini until golden brown
5. Serve when ready

MORNING CHEESE PANINI

Serves: **2**
Prep Time: **5** Minutes

Cook Time: **5** Minutes

Total Time: **10** Minutes

INGREDIENTS

- 2 eggs
- ¼ tsp salt
- 2 tablespoons chives
- 2 bagels
- 3-4 slices tomato
- 3-4 slices onion
- 2 slices ham
- 2 slices ham

DIRECTIONS

1. **Prepare bread for the panini**

2. Place all the ingredients on a bread slice
3. Top with the other bread slice
4. Toast panini until golden brown
5. Serve when ready

SIMPLE PANINI

Serves: 2
Prep Time: 5   Minutes
Cook Time: 5   Minutes
Total Time: **10** Minutes

INGREDIENTS

- 1 fried egg
- 2 tablespoons butter
- 1 slice ham
- 2 slices bacon

DIRECTIONS

1. Prepare bread for the panini
2. Place all the ingredients on a bread slice
3. Top with the other bread slice
4. Toast panini until golden brown
5. Serve when ready

TURKEY PANINI

Serves: **2**
Prep Time: **5** Minutes
Cook Time: **5** Minutes
Total Time: **10** Minutes

INGREDIENTS

- 2 slices bread
- 2 tablespoons mayonnaise
- 2 tablespoons guacamole
- 2 slices cheese
- 2 slices tomato

DIRECTIONS

1. Prepare bread for the panini
2. Place all the ingredients on a bread slice
3. Top with the other bread slice
4. Toast panini until golden brown

5. Serve when ready

WAFFLE PANINI

Serves: **2**
Prep Time: **5** Minutes
Cook Time: **5** Minutes
Total Time: **10** Minutes

INGREDIENTS

- 2 waffles
- 2 eggs
- 2 tablespoon butters
- 2 slices cheddar cheese
- 2 breakfast sausage

DIRECTIONS

1. Prepare bread for the panini
2. Place all the ingredients on a bread slice
3. Top with the other bread slice
4. Toast panini until golden brown

5. Serve when ready

KIDS PANINI

Serves: **2**
Prep Time: **5** Minutes
Cook Time: **5** Minutes
Total Time: **10** Minutes

INGREDIENTS

- 4 slices bread
- 4 eggs
- 2 oz. cheddar cheese
- 1 mango
- 2 tablespoons salsa

DIRECTIONS

1. Prepare bread for the panini
2. Place all the ingredients on a bread slice
3. Top with the other bread slice
4. Toast panini until golden brown

5. Serve when ready

BISTRO PANINI

Serves: **2**
Prep Time: **5**   Minutes
Cook Time: **5**   Minutes
Total Time: **10**   Minutes

INGREDIENTS

- 4 bacon strips
- 2 tsp butter
- 4 eggs
- 4 slices bread
- ¼ tsp salt
- 4 oz. cheese
- ¼ cup baby spinach

DIRECTIONS

1. Prepare bread for the panini
2. Place all the ingredients on a bread slice

3. Top with the other bread slice
4. Toast panini until golden brown
5. Serve when ready

SIMPLE PANINI

Serves: 2
Prep Time: 5   Minutes
Cook Time: 5   Minutes
Total Time: 10   Minutes

INGREDIENTS

- 2 slices bread
- 2 tsp butter
- 2 tablespoon cheese
- 2 bacon slices

DIRECTIONS

1. Prepare bread for the panini
2. Place all the ingredients on a bread slice
3. Top with the other bread slice
4. Toast panini until golden brown
5. Serve when ready

BRUNCH PANINI

Serves: **2**
Prep Time: **5**   Minutes
Cook Time: **5**   Minutes
Total Time: **10** Minutes

INGREDIENTS

- 6 oz. provolone cheese
- 4 slices bread
- 8 slices prosciutto
- 4 eggs
- ¼ berry jam
- 2 tablespoons butter

DIRECTIONS

1. Prepare bread for the panini
2. Place all the ingredients on a bread slice
3. Top with the other bread slice

4. Toast panini until golden brown
5. Serve when ready

BREAKFAST BAGEL PANINI

Serves: **2**
Prep Time: **5**   Minutes
Cook Time: **5**   Minutes
Total Time: **10**   Minutes

INGREDIENTS

- 2 eggs
- 2 bagels
- 2 tablespoons mayonnaise
- 2 slices cheese
- 4 slices prosciutto

DIRECTIONS

1. Prepare bread for the panini
2. Place all the ingredients on a bread slice
3. Top with the other bread slice
4. Toast panini until golden brown

5. Serve when ready

BISCUIT PANINI

Serves: **2**
Prep Time: **5**   Minutes

Cook Time: **5**   Minutes

Total Time: **10**   Minutes

INGREDIENTS

- 2 fried eggs
- 2 slices bacon
- 2 biscuits
- 2 cheese slices
- 2 bread slices

DIRECTIONS

1. Prepare bread for the panini
2. Place all the ingredients on a bread slice
3. Top with the other bread slice
4. Toast panini until golden brown

5. Serve when ready

CHOCOLATE PANINI

Serves: **2**
Prep Time: **5** Minutes

Cook Time: **5** Minutes

Total Time: **10** Minutes

INGREDIENTS

- 2 slices bread
- 2 oz. chopped chocolate

DIRECTIONS

1. Prepare bread for the panini
2. Place all the ingredients on a bread slice
3. Top with the other bread slice
4. Toast panini until golden brown
5. Serve when ready

BANANA PANINI

Serves: **2**
Prep Time: **5**   Minutes
Cook Time: **5**   Minutes
Total Time: **10**   Minutes

INGREDIENTS

- 2 slices bread
- 1 banana slices
- 2 oz. chocolate

DIRECTIONS

1. Prepare bread for the panini
2. Place all the ingredients on a bread slice
3. Top with the other bread slice
4. Toast panini until golden brown
5. Serve when ready

STRAWBERRY PANINI

Serves: 2
Prep Time: 5   Minutes
Cook Time: 5   Minutes
Total Time: *10*   Minutes

INGREDIENTS

- 2 slices bread
- 1 banana sliced
- 2 oz. strawberry

DIRECTIONS

1. Prepare bread for the panini
2. Place all the ingredients on a bread slice
3. Top with the other bread slice
4. Toast panini until golden brown
5. Serve when ready

PEANUT BUTTER PANINI

Serves: 2
Prep Time: 5   Minutes
Cook Time: 5   Minutes
Total Time: *10*   Minutes

INGREDIENTS

- 2 slices bread
- 1 banana sliced
- 2 tablespoons peanut butter

DIRECTIONS

1. Prepare bread for the panini
2. Place all the ingredients on a bread slice
3. Top with the other bread slice
4. Toast panini until golden brown
5. Serve when ready

PINEAPPLE PANINI

Serves: **2**
Prep Time: **5**   Minutes
Cook Time: **5**   Minutes
Total Time: **10** Minutes

INGREDIENTS

- 2 slices bread
- 2 oz. strawberry
- 2 oz. pineapple

DIRECTIONS

1. Prepare bread for the panini
2. Place all the ingredients on a bread slice
3. Top with the other bread slice
4. Toast panini until golden brown
5. Serve when ready

BLUEBERRY PANINI

Serves: 2
Prep Time: 5   Minutes
Cook Time: 5   Minutes
Total Time: *10*   Minutes

INGREDIENTS

- 2 slices bread
- 1 banana sliced
- 3 oz. blueberries
- 2 oz. strawberries

DIRECTIONS

1. Prepare bread for the panini
2. Place all the ingredients on a bread slice
3. Top with the other bread slice
4. Toast panini until golden brown
5. Serve when ready

APPLE PANINI

Serves: **2**
Prep Time: **5**   Minutes

Cook Time: **5**   Minutes

Total Time: **10** Minutes

INGREDIENTS

- 2 slices bread
- 1 tablespoon raspberry jam
- 3-4 apple slices

DIRECTIONS

1. Prepare bread for the panini
2. Place all the ingredients on a bread slice
3. Top with the other bread slice
4. Toast panini until golden brown
5. Serve when ready

PEAR PANINI

Serves: **2**

Prep Time: **5**   Minutes

Cook Time: **5**   Minutes

Total Time: **10**   Minutes

INGREDIENTS

- 2 slices bread
- 1 tablespoon raspberry jam
- 3-4 slices pear

DIRECTIONS

1. Prepare bread for the panini
2. Place all the ingredients on a bread slice
3. Top with the other bread slice
4. Toast panini until golden brown
5. Serve when ready

SALAMI PANINI

Serves: **2**

Prep Time: **5**   Minutes

Cook Time: **5**   Minutes

Total Time: **10**   Minutes

INGREDIENTS

- 3-4 slices salami
- 2 fried eggs
- ¼ cup red peppers
- ¼ cup arugula
- 3-4 slices cheese
- 4 bread slices

DIRECTIONS

1. Prepare bread for the panini
2. Place all the ingredients on a bread slice
3. Top with the other bread slice

4. Toast panini until golden brown
5. Serve when ready

APRICOTS PANINI

Serves: **2**
Prep Time: **5** Minutes
Cook Time: **5** Minutes

Total Time: **10** Minutes

INGREDIENTS

- 1 tablespoon butter
- 4-5 tablespoons mascarpone cheese
- 4 bread slices
- 1 cup apricots
- ¼ cup dried cherries

DIRECTIONS

1. Prepare bread for the panini
2. Place all the ingredients on a bread slice
3. Top with the other bread slice
4. Toast panini until golden brown

5. Serve when ready

BACON RANCH PANINI

Serves: **2**
Prep Time: **5**   Minutes

Cook Time: **5**   Minutes

Total Time: **10**   Minutes

INGREDIENTS

- 4 slices bread
- 4 tablespoons butter
- 1 chicken breast
- 1 tablespoon mustard
- 4 slices bacon
- 4 slices cheddar cheese

DIRECTIONS

1. Prepare bread for the panini
2. Place all the ingredients on a bread slice
3. Top with the other bread slice

4. Toast panini until golden brown
5. Serve when ready

EGGPLANT PANINI

Serves: *2*
Prep Time: *5*   Minutes

Cook Time: *5*   Minutes

Total Time: *10* Minutes

INGREDIENTS

- 1 eggplant
- ¼ tsp salt
- 4 bread slices
- 4 slices mozzarella cheese
- 2 tablespoons pesto
- 3-4 slices tomato

DIRECTIONS

1. Prepare bread for the panini
2. Place all the ingredients on a bread slice
3. Top with the other bread slice

4. Toast panini until golden brown
5. Serve when ready

CHICKPEAS PANINI

Serves: **2**
Prep Time: **5**   Minutes

Cook Time: **5**   Minutes

Total Time: **10**   Minutes

INGREDIENTS

- 4 bread slices
- 8 oz. chickpeas
- 2 tablespoons tahini
- 1 cup dried tomatoes
- 1 red bell pepper
- 1 zucchini
- 1 onion

DIRECTIONS

1. Prepare bread for the panini
2. Place all the ingredients on a bread slice

3. Top with the other bread slice
4. Toast panini until golden brown
5. Serve when ready

VEGETARIAN PANINI

Serves: **2**
Prep Time: **5** Minutes

Cook Time: **5** Minutes

Total Time: **10** Minutes

INGREDIENTS

- 1 cup red bell pepper
- 2 onion slices
- 2 tomato slices
- 2 tablespoon goat cheese
- 1 tablespoon thyme
- ¼ tsp black pepper
- 4 bread slices

DIRECTIONS

1. Prepare bread for the panini
2. Place all the ingredients on a bread slice

3. Top with the other bread slice
4. Toast panini until golden brown
5. Serve when ready

CAULIFLOWER CURRY PANINI

Serves: **2**
Prep Time: **5**   Minutes
Cook Time: **5**   Minutes

Total Time: **10** Minutes

INGREDIENTS

- **2 tsp tamarind paste**
- **¼ cup roasted cauliflower**
- **3-4 slices roasted potato**
- **1 tsp curry powder**
- **¼ tsp turmeric**
- **¼ cup peas**
- **8 oz. chickpeas**
- **4 bread slices**

DIRECTIONS

1. **Prepare bread for the panini**

2. Place all the ingredients on a bread slice
3. Top with the other bread slice
4. Toast panini until golden brown
5. Serve when ready

PESTO PANINI

Serves: **2**
Prep Time: **5** Minutes
Cook Time: **5** Minutes
Total Time: **10** Minutes

INGREDIENTS

- 4 bread slices
- 1 cup pesto
- 6 tomato slices
- 2 tablespoons butter

DIRECTIONS

1. Prepare bread for the panini
2. Place all the ingredients on a bread slice
3. Top with the other bread slice
4. Toast panini until golden brown
5. Serve when ready

GRILLED CHEESE PANINI

Serves: **2**
Prep Time: **5** Minutes
Cook Time: **5** Minutes
Total Time: **10** Minutes

INGREDIENTS

- 4 bread slices
- 4 oz. mozzarella
- 2 oz. feta cheese
- 2 tsp basil
- 2 tablespoons butter

DIRECTIONS

1. Prepare bread for the panini
2. Place all the ingredients on a bread slice
3. Top with the other bread slice
4. Toast panini until golden brown

5. Serve when ready

CAPRESE PANINI

Serves: **2**
Prep Time: **5** Minutes
Cook Time: **5** Minutes
Total Time: **10** Minutes

INGREDIENTS

- 4 bread slices
- 1 tomato
- 4 slices mozzarella cheese
- ¼ cup basil leaves
- 1 tsp olive oil

DIRECTIONS

1. Prepare bread for the panini
2. Place all the ingredients on a bread slice
3. Top with the other bread slice
4. Toast panini until golden brown

5. Serve when ready

GOAT CHEESE PANINI

Serves: **2**
Prep Time: **5**   Minutes
Cook Time: **5**   Minutes
Total Time: **10** Minutes

INGREDIENTS

- 4 bread slices
- 2 oz. goat cheese
- ¼ cup baby spinach
- ½ cup red peppers
- 2 tablespoons butter

DIRECTIONS

1. Prepare bread for the panini
2. Place all the ingredients on a bread slice
3. Top with the other bread slice
4. Toast panini until golden brown

5. Serve when ready

MEDITERRANEAN PANINI

Serves: **2**
Prep Time: **5**   Minutes
Cook Time: **5**   Minutes
Total Time: **10** Minutes

INGREDIENTS

- 4 bread slices
- 1 zucchini
- 4 slices cheese
- ½ cup red peppers
- ¼ cup basil leaves

DIRECTIONS

1. Prepare bread for the panini
2. Place all the ingredients on a bread slice
3. Top with the other bread slice
4. Toast panini until golden brown

5. Serve when ready

BEANS AND BACON PANINI

Serves: **2**
Prep Time: **5**   Minutes

Cook Time: **5**   Minutes

Total Time: **10**   Minutes

INGREDIENTS

- 4 bread slices
- 4 slices bacon
- 2 tablespoon barbeque sauce
- 6-8 oz. baked beans
- 4 slices cheese

DIRECTIONS

1. Prepare bread for the panini
2. Place all the ingredients on a bread slice
3. Top with the other bread slice
4. Toast panini until golden brown

5. Serve when ready

PROSCIUTTO PANINI

Serves: **2**
Prep Time: **5** Minutes
Cook Time: **5** Minutes
Total Time: **10** Minutes

INGREDIENTS

- 4 bread slices
- ¼ tsp black pepper
- 8 oz. prosciutto
- 8 oz. swiss cheese
- 2 fried eggs

DIRECTIONS

1. Prepare bread for the panini
2. Place all the ingredients on a bread slice
3. Top with the other bread slice
4. Toast panini until golden brown

5. Serve when ready

PORK PANINI

Serves: **2**
Prep Time: **5**   Minutes

Cook Time: **5**   Minutes

Total Time: **10**   Minutes

INGREDIENTS

- 4 bread slices
- 4 pork chops
- ¼ cup pesto
- 4 oz. provolone cheese

DIRECTIONS

1. Prepare bread for the panini
2. Place all the ingredients on a bread slice
3. Top with the other bread slice
4. Toast panini until golden brown
5. Serve when ready

SMOKED TURKEY PANINI

Serves: 2
Prep Time: 5   Minutes

Cook Time: 5   Minutes

Total Time: *10*   Minutes

INGREDIENTS

- 4 bread slices
- 8 slices bacon
- 8 slices smoked turkey
- 4 oz. mayonnaise
- 2 cups baby spinach

DIRECTIONS

1. Prepare bread for the panini
2. Place all the ingredients on a bread slice
3. Top with the other bread slice
4. Toast panini until golden brown

5. Serve when ready

FONTINA PANINI

Serves: 2
Prep Time: 5   Minutes
Cook Time: 5   Minutes
Total Time: 10 Minutes

INGREDIENTS

- 4 bread slices
- 4 slices bacon
- 2 tablespoons mustard
- 8 oz. fontina cheese
- 1 red bell pepper

DIRECTIONS

1. Prepare bread for the panini
2. Place all the ingredients on a bread slice
3. Top with the other bread slice
4. Toast panini until golden brown

5. Serve when ready

BRIE PANINI

Serves: **2**
Prep Time: **5**   Minutes
Cook Time: **5**   Minutes
Total Time: ***10***   Minutes

INGREDIENTS

- 4 bread slices
- 1 chicken breast
- 1 onion
- 4 slices bacon
- 4 slices brie cheese
- ¼ cup parsley

DIRECTIONS

1. Prepare bread for the panini
2. Place all the ingredients on a bread slice
3. Top with the other bread slice

4. Toast panini until golden brown
5. Serve when ready

Serves: 2
Prep Time: 5   Minutes
Cook Time: 5   Minutes
Total Time: 10   Minutes

INGREDIENTS

- 4 bread slices
- 2 slices provolone cheese
- 3-4 slices avocado
- 2 tsp pesto
- ¼ cup spinach
- 4-5 tomato slices

DIRECTIONS

1. Prepare bread for the panini
2. Place all the ingredients on a bread slice
3. Top with the other bread slice

4. Toast panini until golden brown
5. Serve when ready

STEAK PANINI

Serves: **2**

Prep Time: **5** Minutes

Cook Time: **5** Minutes

Total Time: ***10*** Minutes

INGREDIENTS

- 4 bread slices
- 2 rib eye steaks
- 4 fried eggs
- 1 tablespoon parsley
- 4 tablespoons butter
- 4 slices cheddar cheese

DIRECTIONS

1. Prepare bread for the panini
2. Place all the ingredients on a bread slice
3. Top with the other bread slice

4. Toast panini until golden brown
5. Serve when ready

THANK YOU FOR READING THIS BOOK!

CPSIA information can be obtained
at www.ICGtesting.com
Printed in the USA
LVHW092326080320
649334LV00001BA/162